Simply My Thoughts

One Moment at a Time

Felicia TaMar Urquhart

ISBN: 978-1-955312-19-6

Printed in the United States of America
Story Corner Publishing & Consulting, Inc.
1510 Atlanta Ave.
Portsmouth, VA 23704

Storycornerpublishing@yahoo.com
www.StoryCornerPublishing.com

Dedication

*I dedicate this book to the memory of my parents,
His Eminence, Bishop Abraham H. Urquhart, and
Mother Harriet M. Urquhart.
Thank you, God, for the ability to write with the power of ink.*

Acknowledgments

Simply My Thank you!

During this journey, so many stood in the gap praying for me, who kept me uplifted before God, and for this, I say thank you. However, there is one particular young lady that I want to say "thank you" to, and she is my daughter, Vernicia Joi Urquhart. Thank you, my baby, for encouraging and pushing me beyond my boundaries. You believed in me when there was no belief in myself; you even were the "motherly voice" in my ear that was needed on so many occasions. When God entrusted you with me, I was extremely nervous and terrified; but to look at you now, at the phenomenal woman you have become, I am convinced that God knew what He was doing.

Thank you, Vee, for the motivation to not give up, to not quit or surrender to my imperfections but to embrace them and use them to bring greatness out of me. I am no longer afraid to speak through my writing for myself because of you.

Table of content

Forward

I have known Felicia for the better part of thirty years. I have seen her during the highs and lows of her life, as a musician, a mother, a preacher, and as a daughter. Undoubtedly each phase of life will take us all into various reflective moments where we "talk to ourselves." I am confident that each of us has to honestly admit that at some point, we all have inner conversations that no one else is privy to hear. Dependent upon the outcome of the discussion will then ultimately reflect certain behaviors or attitudes.

Some of our reflections will be remembered for future contemplation; thus, putting those thoughts on paper becomes essential. Felicia provides her readers with an inside view of some of her daily reflections. Ideas that some of us may have had ourselves and that will bring a smile to our faces or take us to a deeper place within ourselves to possibly find a remedy for an issue that has been disturbing our peace for some time. I admire her willingness to be transparent and to have all of us understand that no matter how devout we may be in our walk with the Lord, there are those times we are without answers to some of life's most plaguing questions. Yet, it is beautiful to know that we have an all-knowing, all-powerful God who can help provide sure guidance when we feel that we have lost our way. It is refreshing to see how there is no pretense with her desire to share what may even be embarrassing moments with sincerity and open honesty.

Every reader will be blessed beyond measure to take the journey through her thoughts while at the same time visiting places in their mind and life that are glaringly similar. She has taken that which may be somewhat complex and made it—Simply Her Thoughts!!

~Apostle Gilbert Coleman, Jr.~

Simply My Thoughts will lead you on a journey full of exploration and personal self-actualization. It is a revealing work of introspection that answers some of the questions we ponder in search of answers. In light of our current world situations, it is increasingly difficult to know the final destination of these events. Felicia lends a voice to the plethora of thoughts in our minds, covering an array of interjections. Her writings will challenge, provoke, and enlightened the reader one moment at a time.

~Dr. Charlayne Henry, Ph.D. ~

Introduction

Hi there, my name is Felicia, and for so long, I have written articles, resolutions, and letters to and for various people for all kinds of reasons. What can I say? God has given me a unique gift to write the intent of my heart and others. I love my gift! This time I wrote for myself, from my heart and the inward parts of me. You see, there have been so many different challenges in my life; challenges of failure, challenges of despair, challenges of facing fears, and even the challenges of embracing victory and love. This memoir is my first attempt at meeting the challenge of saying to the enemy, no longer will I be bound by what you think I should or should not say.

My writings have brought rejuvenation, reclassification, and restoration. Writing my thoughts down has indeed been a great conversation piece to have with Father God. To you, the reader, thank you for your support—blessings to, for, and over you, for being a blessing to me.

After reading over my thoughts in this book, please take some time to write down your thoughts in the spaces provided. I promise you, as you write, God will give answers to whatever questions or concerns you have. Your answers might come right away, or they might not; but if you keep your heart pure towards God, He will not leave you struggling in your thoughts or with hardening of the heart. These, again, are Simply my Thoughts.

Prologue

As Christians, we often look for answers about ourselves through people, psychics, psychologists, fortune tellers, prophets, and even astrologers. Unfortunately, very few, if ever, look in the mirror and ask the reflection, who am I? How did I get here? Better yet, what is this place? I have never been here before. What am I supposed to do now? I was not like this a few months, years ago; which way do I go? I do not remember me being like this; what happened to me? I was happy with who I was, what I was doing in life, where I was going, and how I achieved my goals. So, why am I not feeling more optimistic? Where did the beat of my drum go?

When you look in the mirror, the problem and the solution look at you in most cases. There are so many ways that the devil revolves around our aura, and the minute that he sees an opening or a weak spot, he becomes like gas and seeps his way into our atmosphere. At first, we do not see it as interference from the devil; we look at it as life. The Apostle Paul asked this question to the church of Galatia, "ye did run well; who did hinder you that ye should not obey the truth?" How many of us will answer this question truthfully? Let me be the first to say, NOT ME! And I did not, not until I took the blinders off my eyes and saw what I had allowed happening to me. You would be amazed at the little things that we thought were not harmful but had a great punch that damaged us beyond measure.

What I reverted to, in addition to prayer, fasting, and studying the Word of God, was writing, simply writing down my thoughts. I found that sometimes when I could not express my hurt, my pains, and my disappointments that the next best thing was to write them down. Being that we live in a world of technology, having a tape recorder is a little outdated, but the power of the ink, always, always, always is in season. I have found that it has been a healing balm, a release, and a relief mechanism. I write this book hoping that you find a relatable word, line, or paragraph that will get you to join me in simply writing your thoughts and passing them forward. Life does have its challenges, but so does this Christian walk. The difference is, life depends on the "ways" of life, and our dependency is based on the "ways" of the Giver of life. It's in Him that we live, breathe, and have our being. I pray that you will identify these writings as a tool to help you keep it honest with yourself and God.

"The LORD bless thee and keep thee; The LORD make His face shine upon thee, and be gracious unto Thee; The LORD lift His countenance upon thee and give thee peace."—Numbers 6:24-26 (KJV)

Thought 1: Simply Fruity
Simply My Thoughts

Everyone knows that I love fruit, and I do, for a lot of reasons, but mainly to help keep my body regulated. Each fruit has its function to help keep you healthy: bananas – potassium; Oranges –Vitamin-C; apples—fiber; grapes—iron, and the list goes on. In St. John chapter 15, Jesus explains how abiding in the vine will produce long-lasting fruit. By the end of the chapter, Jesus says, He chose us so we might bear fruit that would last. Natural fruits are temporary. Spiritual fruits are perpetual. We must eat the fruit that we purchase from the grocery store, or it will decay, but the fruit of the Spirit (Galatians 5:22-23) that is implanted in us by God will never grow or go bad; it is from the GREAT vine, and it will last and last. Today, I employ you to bear good fruits. Let love, joy, peace, longsuffering, gentleness, goodness, faith, meekness, and temperance be imported into someone from you so much so that much more fruit can grow. Spiritual fruit does the Natural body better!

_____

_____

_____

_____

_____

_____

_____

_____

Thought 2: Mind To Waste
Simply My Thoughts

" . . . and the peace of God which passeth all understanding, will keep your heart and mind through Christ Jesus." Some time ago, I preached that "Quitting is not an option"; well, today, I say, losing your mind isn't one either! Paul said to Timothy, "God has not given us the spirit of fear, but of power, love and a sound mind" (II Timothy 1:7 KJV). So, if God has given us a SOUND mind, then at no given time does this mind get lost. The perfect peace of God keeps us together, from head to toe. It is the devil's tactic to bombard the mind with "what ifs" in the negative sense, but God takes the "what ifs" and says, "what is." God, I got it. What you want us to do is simple. We must feed our minds with what we know to be true, and that is, the devil is defeated, God is exalted, and we have achieved victory in this place.

> *The Perfect peace of God keeps us together, from head to toe.*

Thought 3: Do Due
Simply My Thoughts

Goodness gracious, the season of manifestation is here. Everything that God said that WE would be, have, and accomplish is coming to pass this season. This is the DO and DUE season. Everything due to us will come to us without hast, without complication, and without interference. Continue to seek Him and do what is required of you spiritually and naturally. Now, understand that the devil is not going to sit back and let you ride easy. Oh no!! But the WORD will be your guide, your shield, your buckler, and your defense. Your pathway will be bright, and your walkway will be straight. There is no tactic that the devil can create that will change your course or have your course be changed. Keep your focus. Stand on the WORD of God!! For He knows what He has in stored for you, and it will come to pass. Believe, and you will receive!!

_____

_____

_____

_____

_____

_____

_____

_____

Thought 4: His Word- A Mystery
Simply My Thoughts

So, we have arrived at the last Sunday of this 2020 year. A year that people, including me, have declared to be filled with witchcraft, despair, and hardship because of the pandemic (COVID-19). Isn't it amazing how a lot of the saints believed their fate to be filled with struggle and strife because of "repeated" rumors of "war" and "doom," when God proved Himself mighty not only to the believers but to the unbelievers as well? Yes, a declaration of recession filled the air, but God promised that He would provide. I am encouraged to know and believe that He brought us through the year to prove that it's not in a number, and neither is it on human predictions. His WORD is a mystery, but it is true! It cannot lie; it must fulfill the destiny that it has been assigned.

I encourage all of us to move forward into the New Year with declarations of God's WORD.
"Lo, I am with you always, even unto the end of the earth."

_____
_____
_____
_____
_____
_____
_____
_____

"His WORD is a mystery, but it's true!"

Thought 5: Press To Push
Simply My Thoughts

Today, my thoughts are geared towards young people. 2021 has entered with a roar for some of you; yet, you haven't thrown in the towel. I thank God for your determination not to be defeated. With compromising situations meeting you at your front door, the struggle is seriously real. I see you in the neighborhood, waiting on the bus, walking in the malls, or just to the corner store and the devil sniffing you out. As it is with the adults, you, too, are fighting a war that God will give you the grace, strength, and wisdom to sustain and be victorious.

> *You must keep pressing if you want more of GOD!*

Young lady, young man, I am so Godly proud of you for your efforts thus far; however, you, too, must take it up a notch. There is more to GO through and to GROW through. You must keep pressing if you want more of God. Continue to be faithful in your serving, in reading the WORD, and in acknowledging HIM in ALL your WAYS. Don't be discouraged by what you see, hear or feel; keep fasting and praying for HE will never leave you nor forsake you, and neither will I. (smile) I'm praying for and with you.

_____

_____

_____

_____

_____

_____

_____

_____

Thought 6: Latter Is Greater
Simply My Thoughts

This morning I encourage myself, my own heart as I grow and go in God. The enemy wants me to think that I'm not worthy of the abundance that God has for me, that I'm not ready or prepared to move forward in newness. NOT only am I prepared, but God has prepared me and the way. God said, "Remain watchful and prayerful. The enemy will pull out all stops; use anyone and anything to hinder you from receiving this abundance. Do not let him!!! Stay connected to the source, stay on your knees, and do not give up nor give in. No matter what or how things look, believe God!!" Isa 45:2 assures us that "God will go before us and make the crooked places straight and break in pieces the gates of bronze and cut the bars of iron." This is our reassurance, people of God, that He is our "hammer," and He is removing the rocks and stones in your way. The walls are coming down. Get ready; better days are coming, for your latter shall be greater than your past. God, I receive this; thank you.

_____

_____

_____

_____

_____

_____

_____

_____

Thought 7: Haters Validate
Simply My Thoughts

I have learned, like David, to encourage myself in the LORD. You know, folk are going to talk whether it's for good or bad, not realizing that their talk might be harmful, but it's more helpful than anything. What are you saying, Elder? Let your haters validate you!! That is all it is. You are not doing anything to them. Like Daniel, he was a good man, clean, friendly, stayed out of trouble, treated everybody right, was just the ordinary guy loving him some God. Prayed, fasted, and honored the Lord in all his ways. He received a promotion, became a leader, and the haters sought to find something wrong with him; but they could not. So, they did the right thing, according to the king, but for the wrong reasons. Wrong motives will backfire every time. The end result for Daniel's haters wasn't a pat on the back or a better promotion; it was Daniel's VICTORY in the lion's den. They validated his testimony of who he was—the KING's kid. So, let them talk and recognize that you, too, are the KING's kid. I AM a King's Kid!

> *Let your haters validate you*

_____

_____

_____

_____

_____

_____

_____

Thought 8: Write, Write, And Write Some More
Simply My Thoughts

David said in Psalm 127:1, "Except the LORD build the house, they labor in vain that build it; except the LORD keep the city, the watchman waketh but in vain." As God speaks, I write, and He is saying that the direction that the LORD is taking us this year requires strategic planning, purposeful planning, and precise determination. God will give us an increase, so much so that we will buy and build. We will expand—not only in people, but in knowledge, in worship, in prayer, and our praise. We are seriously embarking upon the continuation of supernatural overflow, supernatural deliverance, and the abundance of supernatural healing. We must accomplish everything in God's way. God has the master plan, so we do not have to wonder how, why, when, or where; no, we simply need to do what is required of us, and everything else will be provided and added. Write the vision, make it plain, and run!!!

_____

_____

_____

_____

_____

_____

_____

_____

Thought 9: Rise Above It
Simply My Thoughts

God is calling His people to go deeper in Him, to seek to know His moves, His ways, His voice, His guidance, His strength, His direction, and His wisdom. Are we willing to go that far? As I sit here in my office, I ask myself, "How far do I want to go? How much do I want to "position" myself in Him? Am I sure that I can commit to the requirements that will be asked of me?" Have you ever asked yourself these questions? Be honest. The more I write, the more my thirst for righteousness' sake is unquenchable.

I desire and want more, so I will go to the furthest extreme to reach the "deep" parts of God. Zacchaeus knew that someone was coming that he needed to see to glean knowledge from them and grow. People were getting in his way, becoming distracting, talking negatively, but his determination spoke loudly in his actions. He climbed the sycamore tree. He did what others did not think to do, and that was to rise above the interference. That is where I am, rising above the distraction and interference so that I can go deep. Do you want to go deep? Then go up, and He will call you to Himself . . . into the depths of Him.

_____

_____

_____

_____

_____

_____

_____

Rise above the interference......

Thought 10: Challenge The Challenge
Simply My Thoughts

How often do you see yourself doing something great for the Kingdom, and suddenly because you do not see results, you decide to give up? Today, God is asking you to challenge the challenge.

Believe in the impossible. Ignite your faith. Do not doubt! Declare that no matter what it looks like, you believe in God (Acts 27:25). The assignments that God gives us are designed to be fulfilled and passed with flying colors. He never issues a task knowing that you will fail. Oh no, He is not that kind of teacher. "Believe in the Lord your God so shall ye be established. Believe His prophets so shall you prosper" (2 Chronicles 20:20 KJV). People of God, you can do great exploits for Him. Let everything that you do bring glory, honor, and praise to God!! If He has approved the blueprint, rest assured He will provide the tenacity to bring the plan together for His Glory and His Kingdom.

_____

_____

_____

_____

_____

_____

_____

_____

Thought 11: God Is... Now
Simply My Thoughts

God is faithful in everything that He says and does. He is faithful to His Word, He never fails, and He is always on time. As the end of the year rapidly approaches, let us take a few minutes and reflect on where we were (relationship-wise) with God and where we are now, and then be bold to say, the Lord has indeed been good to me!! It is human nature to declare our status of living based on what we are experiencing or going through within the now, but the truth of the matter is, God is our NOW. The things that we go through, the experiences that have occurred (naturally/ spiritually), have been for our benefit, to make us who we are NOW. God did, has, and will continue to make us promises, but before manifesting the promise, there is a process. He will make good on the promise that He has made, but you must persevere in the process. Jeremiah 29:11 clearly states that He knows what His plans are for us and that it is to give us an expected end.

Thought 12: Just Smile
Simply My Thoughts

So today, as I sojourned to work, the bus driver gave me such a strange look. And being a little perplexed, I asked, "Why are you looking at me as though I have not washed my face?" His response was, "Ma'am, what kind of look is that?" A little confused, I realized he was talking about my cheerful expression. I asked him why it mattered, and he explained with a frown that it just stood out from the others riding the bus that day. I responded, "Oh well, it's just how I'm feeling." I then added, "Your day will get better, too, if you just smile." His response was not favorable. However, I decided to choose to be the antidote that, through Christ, he needed. Long story short, my last comment to him was, "you will remember me all day, and you will smile." Again, he disagreed, but as I reached my stop to get off, I said to him, "Have a good day." He, in return, asked for my name. I told him, and he told me his with a smile. The moral of this story is that sometimes, it takes a smile to wipe away someone's irritability, mood swing, or "just not a good start to a good day" syndrome. If you were able to wake up, breathe, move, speak, clean your body, and eat food, that alone is enough of a reason to smile. Being grateful for the ability to do should be enough to—SMILE!! Oh, I am pretty sure that during this day, he remembered me.

_____

_____

_____

_____

_____

_____

Just smile......

Thought 13: What's Your Response
Simply My Thoughts

People often respond to the question of "how are you doing?" or "how are you feeling?" with "I can't complain." Today, I thought about that response and how often I have said that, but what do I mean? What is it that I want to say? Was I saying, "I don't like my life because of this, that or another?" or was I singing the "should've, could've, and would've" blues? One thing for sure and two for certain, it was not a response of being grateful for what I had already obtained. Paul stated that in whatever state he was in, he found himself to be content. How many of us are like Paul? To my knowledge, Paul did not complain; but what he did do instead was improve himself. He acknowledged his strengths and weaknesses but expressed the desire to do and want more.

Today, I want more. Today, I will do more. Today, I am more. I accept the things I cannot change. I will change the things that I can and understand the difference between the two. What about you? What will your response be the next time you are asked how you are feeling? I know my response will be—I am content!!

_____

_____

_____

_____

_____

_____

_____

_____

Thought 14: The Road Less Traveled
Simply My Thoughts

Often, we wonder what the LORD requires us to do. And in our wondering, we tend to put what we think into action and say that it is of the LORD. Have you asked God, "what is it that you have for me to do today?" It is imperative, in this Christian walk, that we ask, seek, and learn His will, His way, and His works.

Our ways are not His ways, and neither are our thoughts His thoughts. God's thought process far surpasses our imagination and understanding. So, what I find myself doing is staying in His presence and sitting quietly to hear what He has to say, not only for me but for those that I will encounter during my day. Solomon put it all so plainly in Proverbs 3:4-6 (KJV), "Trust in the Lord with all thy heart and lean not unto thy understanding. In all thy ways acknowledge him, and He shall direct your path." Stop taking the low road and stay on the road that will lead you higher than yourself.

Thought 15: Unconditional Love
Simply My Thoughts

Today, I am grateful for unconditional love. A love that surpasses all understanding; it never tires, nor does it ever weaken. It doesn't get mad when it can't have its way but strengthens me when I need to make a way. I love this kind of love because it makes me appreciate that at any given time, things could be different. Instead of being happy and filled with joy, sadness could be my portion, and doom, depression, despair could be my results. To enjoy smiling and laughing is a much better emotion to display than a frown or a tear. It's better for the body. Did you know that you use more muscles frowning, stressing, and crying than you would if you were to relax, think positive, speak positive and smile? Where can you get this kind of love for yourself?

There is no greater love than this that a man would lay down his life for a friend. I did not know that we were friends until 44 years ago. He was friends with me before I ever knew that I existed. Oh, what love He gives to me, consistently and constantly. His name is Jesus . . . the Righteous Son of God, the Lily of the Valley, and He is the Bright and Morning star. He is my everything. I am not selfish; I'll share Him with you. He has so much love to give; no one, absolutely no one, will ever go lacking.

Thought 16: Time Vs. Time
Simply My Thoughts

Time is the point or period when something occurs—an appointed, fixed, or customary moment or hour for something to happen, begin or end. Time is the only element that can meet and greet itself regardless of where you place it. You can look back into it and refer to it as PAST time; you can look at it now and refer to it as the PRESENT time; you can look ahead and call it the FUTURE time. And then, somewhere in between all of this, there is a MEAN time, which in most cases occurs during a waiting period or a processing period. Regardless of where time may be placed, when the segment is finished and fulfilled, then that place becomes the LAST time. Oddly enough, each adjective puts you in a position of choice. There is a sense of will for us to make time favorable or unfavorable for our destiny. Be it spiritual or natural. If nothing else, in the past year, we were shown that time is not to be wasted, procrastinated, or even depended upon. What we found out is that the Past time had no more dwelling time; the Present time is now cherishing time; and the Future is not, by any means, promised time; however, the Last time stepped, up to the plate, made its presence known, and declared results for us such as the last time to see or hear loved ones, the last time that we would have a job, the last time that we would be able to speak to each other face to face freely, but what the Last time could not declare or even dictate where the blessings of the LORD. The blessings of the LORD it maketh (eth—continuously, over and over again) rich, and He addeth no sorrow with it. Every new day is a new time. It is a time to laugh, time to pray, and time to breathe, a time to walk, talk, and enjoy challenges. Yes, you read right. Enjoy the results of difficulties because time (God) is on your side.

Today, understanding that the scary places of the processes of time are not there to dishearten you, but to strengthen your heart to trust, to love, to cherish, and to acknowledge that your time is in His hands. What time is it for you?

_____

_____

_____

_____

_____

_____

_____

_____

Thought 17: Do It Afraid
Simply My Thoughts

Sometimes you must jump. Take that leap of faith. Sometimes even in being afraid and scared, you have to jump. I understand that we, in human form, are used to something being under our feet; something to feel; something secure, foundational . . . but faith says, my feet are dangling, but I know that I will land on destiny's ground. My feet are dangling, but I know that when I land, wherever my feet trod, I can claim it to be mine. I can use that platform as a foundation to whatever I see as the catapult to my vision, dream, drive, determination, purpose, and goal. When you decide to stop accepting the naysayer's negativity and their belligerence concerning your future; when you choose to get out of your head and your feelings; when you decide that your focus is the betterment of you through God, it is then that the doors of deliverance will not just open, but they will swing open. We have to stop being afraid of the answered prayer that we categorize as "unanswered." Yeah, that part. God has answered prayer after prayer after prayer. Still, for fear of the unknown, we do not acknowledge, respond, or receive that He has already fixed it, that He has already blessed it, that He has already made a way,

> *...stop being afraid of the answered prayer that we have categorized as unanswered*

delivered us, and has set us free. So, what I am going to start doing is stop looking at how far to jump; I'm just going to jump and trust that He will make sure that I land right on time and on target.

_____

_____

_____

_____

_____

Thought 18: Posture Is Everything
Simply My Thoughts

There will come a time that you will be or feel, at your lowest or what you would consider being the lowest point of your life; the key is not to let your lowest make you hit rock bottom, even if it feels like it. But even if that is the inevitable and you hit rock bottom, hit it in the standing position—and remember that it is on Christ, the solid rock you stand for on other grounds you are on sinking sand. When you acknowledge God in everything that you say, do, see, and hear, you will not fall, but you will and can survive on the broken pieces. As I'm writing this, I am reminded that whether or not you break when you bend, that's a decision totally up to you. When we were created, we were not designed to quit. We were made to win, withstand, and weather through. Before we were in our mother's womb, the purpose was already established, the vision was already provided, wisdom was already set in motion, confidence was being nurtured . . . the entire being of human was already being constructed to take on the form of a conqueror. Fearfully and wonderfully made in the likeness of God and the image of Christ—this, to me, is a well-put-together physique. So, even at your lowest, acknowledge Him in ALL your ways, and He will direct your path and lead you to victory. In him, I am always the VICTOR and not the victim!!

_____

_____

_____

_____

_____

_____

_____

Thought 19: Friend For Real
Simply My Thoughts

Friendship what does it mean? What does it do? How is it possible? Where does it come from? Where can I get it? Friendship is truly one of the greatest gifts in life. One who has unreliable friends soon comes to ruin, but a friend sticks closer than a brother (Proverbs 18:24 NIV). This passage of scripture speaks of our Christ Jesus; however, at this moment, I am thinking about my dearest friend of 38 years, who just recently earned her wings to glory. The shared secrets, the truths that were told, the disagreements that took place, and let us not forget the distance of living, the miles between us, never interfered with her commitment to me as a friend. True blue friendships go through some things. You get tested on every angle. If you are trustworthy, honest, sensitive, integral, closed mouth or loose lips will determine if you are compatible with even friends. Obtaining a friend is not hard, not unless you make it hard to be obtainable. Even God has a plan for friendships. One of the requirements is that the ordained friend must stick closer than your brother. Wow!! Friendships have prerequisites. Well, how about that!! If you desire to have friends, you must first show yourself to be friendly. A true friend will check you when you are wrong. They will stand their ground, even when you've turned your back on them, because you're in your feelings. They will love you hard and will always be there. I sit, and I think about how many times I have dropped the ball on my friend(s), and then I think about how many times they have dropped the ball on me. It is a fantastic thing how God takes life experiences to teach you to become better, stronger, more intelligent, more honest, and more genuine. With love and kindness, God has drawn us to Him. I believe that He put that strength of love and kindness in the ordinance of friendship. Get God, and you will have a friend. Oh, how I have found this to be true. I must honestly say, in this

Christian journey, if I had not had God in me, there wouldn't be a friend for me. Again, it is something about the nature of the human being. God did not make us perfect for each other, but in fact, He made us perfect in Him. There is not a friend, as the lowly Jesus, no not one, no not one.

_____

_____

_____

_____

_____

_____

_____

_____

Thought 20: Challenged By Weakness
Simply My Thoughts

Have you ever had one of those days that everything just walked up to you and slapped you several times over and over with random stuff? Talking about being in the trenches, a place of protection from danger, a hiding place from the enemy. I have asked myself, how badly do I want the enemy to lose its power? Lose its formation? Lose its hold on me? How badly do I want my freedom, whether financial, mental, physical, emotional, psychological, or spiritual? How bad? How far in the distance will I go to keep my sanity, to live peacefully, to live wholly and Holy? Am I willing to pay the price to live a delivered life? Temptation is a terrible thing, especially when it is in league with its cousin, Vulnerability. Today was one of those days that I just wanted to give in, give up, give away, and surrender to my feelings. I was not thinking about consequences, repercussions, penalties, or any other type of punishment that would result in my giving in to the temptation. Then this thought came to me like a ton of bricks. I must love myself badly enough to get through the temptation. Not just get through the temptation but live through it. Deliverance is not always one and done; not. The devil will come to you with all kinds of stuff. Stuff that you have never considered doing, but if he could get you to do this "one thing, one time," he says, then he will leave you alone. But the truth is, he is a liar, and before you know it, you will have succumbed to that very thing that will knock you back a few steps (years). So, I have learned through the course of this day that deliverance is an ongoing thing. I knew this, but it did not become real until my deliverance was challenged by weakness, a struggle that grabbed me. Yielding, fasting, and praying over yourself daily is what is needed to keep your deliverance on point and keep you in a posture to pray always without ceasing. I got myself together and stood my ground and said, "Although you look good, although it may be fun, although it would be refreshing, I'm not willing to sacrifice the deliverance that I have gained down through the years to be thrown away in hours. Thank you, but no thank you." When I realized that I stood my ground and stood on the Word of God, His WORD is truth. Submit your ways to the LORD, resist the devil and watch as he flees (James 4:7 KJV). That part right there, priceless!

_____
_____
_____
_____
_____
_____
_____
_____
_____

The Word of GOD is TRUTH!

Thought 21: Believe It
Simply My Thoughts

How many times do you preach, teach, share, and tell God's people if you want God to move, provide, and be God? You have got to have faith to believe before you receive that which you desire of the LORD. I used to think that "life" was my enemy. With all that I've gone through, I began to say life isn't fair, but the truth is life is fair and is not my enemy. However, doubt, that distant cousin, now that is a different story, definitely my enemy.

My life is in God's hand, and if I cannot believe that, then I cannot believe in God. Doubt had hardened me to the things that God had promised me, and it would not let me believe in what God had for me. If the devil can keep you in suspense of what God says concerning you, then he will have successfully inducted you into the unbeliever's believers club. If the devil can keep you in suspense, then he will have successfully stopped you from believing the WORD, for he knows your belief in the WORD is what causes your faith to grow. Every day that we get up, we must make sure that the revealed spirit man sits on the seat of our consciousness, and we say let God be true and every man a liar.

When you have faith, your potential cannot be buried. Jesus, the great teacher that HE is and continues to be in the Holy Ghost, simply gave a refresher course to listening, hearing, and applying. Because of my faith, I am going to stay in this race. I must realize that I cannot do it on my intelligence, but I will make it according to my faith. My faith is regulated by His Word and has constraints. Hallelujah!! The cross prohibits me from doing anything that is not of the excellence of God. The excellence of God is where I

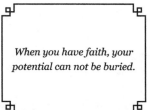

When you have faith, your potential can not be buried.

desire to be; you know, the secret place of His tabernacle where He will hide me.

_____

_____

_____

_____

_____

_____

_____

_____

Thought 22: Don't Get Stuck
Simply My Thoughts

Today, during my quiet time with the LORD, I was so engulfed with God's Word that the words left the page and began drawing the theme of what I was reading into my imagination. Many of us, from time to time, set goals and objectives for where we will be, where we will go, what we will be, and what we will do. Very rarely do we slow down enough to process the plan or acknowledge the plan's purpose. Nor do we expect the plan to turn into His Promises. We become confident in the look of the plan, but we simply ignore the intelligence of the plan. We get caught up or mesmerized by the feel of the outcome versus the stability of the result. We become braggadocios about the idea and use the credit of God as a cover-up to make us look prosperous and anointed so that we would not look foolish. He purposely breathed success over our mess just for the sake of the one that is looking at our life. When I read about Naaman, he was the absolute epitome of a good soldier, right-hand man, leader, and all-out guy. Good-hearted, strong-willed, strong-minded, an intelligent intellectual that was marred on purpose. He was married on the outside. That hit me like a ton of bricks. It does not matter what "goodness" is on the inside; the outward appearance can keep people at a distance to the point that they do not want to get to know the goodness, which in most cases is the natural person. But again, like today's society, because of who he had built himself to believe in, he would not follow a simple instruction to change his outward appearance to match the inside. Wow, talk about time repeating itself. A simple instruction for this world to wear a mask. But because it cramps the style of some, they would rather die than live; they would rather be unsafe than safe or even keep others safe—such a sad commentary. I wonder what it would take for this world to follow the laws of this land; even more so, what would it take for the world to follow Christ. Naaman, eventually, followed the directives of the prophet after he humbled himself to his servant.

I get it, I was raised in the church all my life, and I've seen some things and lost confidence and trust in quite a few folks, but there is always that one person that you will hear, listen, and obey. It is a sad commentary that we stop hearing God through people that we have become familiar with, but that's a horse of another color to talk about at another time. The fact remains that God will use whomever He needs to get you to listen and obey. The outcome will be great. Smooth skin, mended heart, scales lifted from the eyes, uncorked ears, and a smile because there has been a mighty change on the outside that matches the character of change on the inside.

Thought 23: Truth & Consequence
Simply My Thoughts

While preparing myself for my workday, this thought came to me as I was pressing my shirt: You must be open-minded enough to receive what people say before saying that what they are saying is not valid. I have been told repeatedly that I am overly aggressive and demanding, my speaking voice and tone. Of course, when I hear this, I think to myself, "No, I'm not." But today, God brought back to my remembrance a conversation that was held with me. He slow-played it, and I saw what people had been saying. Gee whiz!! As loving, caring, giving, saved, sanctified, and filled with the Holy Ghost as I am, there was still a defense mechanism that I had not been delivered from yet. Oh yeah, preacher or no preacher, deliverance is to be made perfect in Him to minister to others.

Did this truth affect me? Absolutely. The question is, what am I going to do about it? I've shared and talked with people on so many levels about being stuck in what they were used to doing until it has become a character flaw in their disposition. Here I am, one of those people, a character flaw in my disposition. I listened to this conversation again and immediately called the person and apologized. The person said, "Fee, that's okay, that's who you are." I responded that is not who I am!" They chuckled, but I was serious. I began to think, how would I feel if someone talked to me in such a manner? Would I be like this person and say, "Oh, it's okay," or would I ask, "Did you mean to speak like that? Demeaning? Ruthless? Like someone owed you something?"

How would I respond to God if He talked to me like I had talked to them? This perception forced me to look inside myself. Sometimes you must go back and check yourself. You might like what you find, and you might not. I am reminded that I am known by the fruits that I bear (shaking my head). This fruit, the root, must die. When you want to represent Christ in everything that you do, self-inventory is needed; a deep cleansing is necessary; repentance is required. Father, forgive me for the many times that this "flaw" has damaged, hurt, or insulted your image. Forgive me for every time someone walked away from me, wounded by my words, actions, or deeds. Forgive me for not seeing in me or hearing from me what I see in others and hear from others.

Make me over again; make me again into another. Purge me with hyssop, and I shall be clean, wash me, and I shall be whiter than snow. This whole episode made me see, oil or no oil, I am susceptible to making a mistake(s) or contributing to the error, in being someone else's pain, stumbling block, being the cause for someone NOT Christ, being the heartbreak or the tears of someone. Wow! How transparent is that? I wonder how many people would search themselves and speak such truths about themselves and then accept, repent, and ask God to do them over.

Not that I saw myself as a perfect person, but I never saw myself as a mean person. Lord, help me to do better and be better. Teach me what to say and how to say. Teach me how not just to show maturity but to display maturity in my actions, words, and deeds. Just when you think that you have been delivered, that thought comes to mind! Help me, LORD, to die daily.

Thought 24: The Power Of Love
Simply My Thoughts

Love is something shown, spoken, felt, and heard. Love is action personified. It is the only action word that can see your pain and create it, mend your hurt, and cause it, wipe your tears and generate them, cause the response of your thinking to be straight, and have you perplexed all at the same time. Love is strong but not forceful, sensitive but not weak, comforting but not controlling.

Love sees the need, hears the want, speaks the truth, touches the unknown, resurrects the dormancy, and cradles insecurity while massaging the center of the heart as the holding place for it all. Love is the invisible power that can walk through the thickest wall, break through the most challenging foundation, and heal the oldest wound. Love does not give any assurances, but it'll build confidence that you can and will survive, succeed, and sustain. Love can change an intense atmosphere and create an aura of peace and tranquility. Even in the most heated arguments, disagreements or fights, love referees every segment and exterminates every origin of intent and destruction. Love is limitless, courageous, selfless, sweet, kind, never arrogant, and always confident. Experiencing love is a chance taken once in a lifetime that you cherish and hold on to for life.

_____

_____

_____

_____

_____

_____

_____

Thought 25: Thirsting Vs. Thirsty
Simply My Thoughts

Today I experienced an unusual thirst for water. The more water I consumed, the more of a thirst that was needed to be quenched. It seemed that no matter how much I drank, the quantity was not enough. God spoke to me regarding my thirst. "This is how it is with the praises of my people. No matter how much or how often, I never get enough praise from my children. I do not get enough of true worship. When will my people understand that I live in their praises? I operate in and because of their praises. Showers of blessings are disbursed because of the way the house is created for me to live in." God is thirsting for authentic worship, genuine praise, true admiration. Sugarcoating does nothing but increases His desire for purity. It is the same for the human body.

We consume sodas, juices, powered drinks but fail to realize that it never quenches the thirst. Eventually, we will drink water, but when will that happen? After we have been diagnosed as being borderline diabetic or even diabetic because our sugar levels are high? These transparent moments are serious eye-openers. All of this from a thirsting for water? A dry mouth is a sign that something is obscured in the body. It causes many defects to the positioning of your mouth. Why not drink more of the water that will quench the thirsting not only for your natural body but for your spiritual body as well. Naturally, a hydrated body contributes to bone longevity, i.e., teeth, joints, skull, blood vessels; and spiritually, a hydrated body contributes to a sound mind, pure heart, postured position for worship, love, kindness, and so much. Just like this thirst for me today, there is a thirsting just as much for a well of water that will never run dry.

Elder Felicia TaMar Urquhart
About the Author

Elder Felicia TaMar Urquhart is the youngest child of the late Bishop Abraham and Mother Harriett M. Urquhart. Being raised with church protocol was no strange thing to her; however, growing up with the protocol was challenging. Wanting to do like everyone else (outside of the church), the calling on her life (within the church) was more demanding. She accepted Christ, as her Lord and Savior, at the age of 11 years old, under the anointed preaching of her brother, the late Bishop Elwin Marvin Urquhart. From that moment on, understanding the challenge became clear. God had called her unto Himself to His work, His will, His way. Known for her singing, songwriting, and organ playing, the preached word couldn't hide behind these talents any longer. She accepted her calling to preach the gospel, September 1992. Under the leadership of her father, Minister Felicia Urquhart, was groomed and trained for ministry. She attended Maranatha Bible Institute, where she learned the principles of the Gospel. In June of 1997, Minister Felicia was given an Evangelist license with a charge to go and do the works of an evangelist. Evangelist Fee, as she was affectionately called, continued to learn more about her "craft" under the leadership of both Apostle Dorothy B. Lane and Apostle Shelita L. Lane of Franklin, Virginia. She attended the School of Ministry of the Apostolic Faith Church of God Live On, Suffolk, Virginia, under the teachings of Bishop Richard R. Cross, Jr.

In March of 2005, her father summoned her to return to Philadelphia to help him in ministry at Holy Temple Holiness Church. Although her father's health was failing, his spiritual eye saw her works and appointed her an Elder. August of 2006, by the laying on of hands, Bishop J. Shawn Urquhart consecrated her to the office of an Elder in the Lord's Church. From that moment to the present, Elder Felicia Urquhart continues to work in the body of Christ in whatever capacity that's needed. She has served as: Sunday School Secretary, Sunday School Teacher, Sunday School Superintendent, Minister of Music (for several churches of different denominations), an Adjutant, Church Janitor, Financial Secretary, General Secretary, Youth President, and the list goes on and on. Elder Felicia has been a facilitator for several Music, Women, Youth, and Convention Conferences throughout the East Coast. She is the writer and producer of the Christian Stage Play, "Don't Let the Devil Do It" (March 2009). She is a creative and skillful writer.

She has received both her bachelor's and master's degrees in Biblical Studies from the North Carolina College of Theology (Baltimore, MD Satellite Division). Currently, she resides in Baltimore, MD, and attends Trinity New Birth International Ministries under the leadership of Bishop Isabel E. Grant. She is the proud mother of one daughter, Vernicia Joi Urquhart, and spiritual mother to many. She hails from a family legacy of prominent preachers, teachers, pastors, bishops, and psalmists. Elder Urquhart is different and unique but a woman of faith destined for Kingdom success.

CPSIA information can be obtained
at www.ICGtesting.com
Printed in the USA
BVHW042204050821
613761BV00007B/14